MW00637435

HIDDEN INCOME

The Secret Guide To Increasing Your Wealth As A Physical Therapist

Dr. R. Brandon Smith

Hidden Income

The Secret Guide To Increasing Your
Wealth As A Physical Therapist

Dr. R. Brandon Smith

ISBN (Print Edition): 978-1-66787-410-4

ISBN (eBook Edition): 978-1-66787-411-1

TABLE OF CONTENTS

Forward

I want to thank my wife, Kendall, because she has always supported my ambitions, dreams, and goals - even when they seemed crazy, stupid, or unrealistic.

Additionally, I want to thank my business coach, Aaron LeBauer, because his coaching has dramatically accelerated the growth of my own business.

Most importantly, I want to dedicate this book to any Physical Therapist who was told that they should settle for average pay and live a mediocre life. Most PTs choose comfort over growth. I am hoping that this book changes your mindset and acts as a guide in allowing you to choose growth over comfort. By choosing growth, you will be in the top 1% of Physical Therapists!

About The Author

Dr. R. Brandon Smith is a licensed physical therapist turned entrepreneur and investor. He is the creator of the 10 CEU Home Health Mentor Course™ and the founder of the Outside The Box Income and Investing™ Community.

Dr. Smith has helped over 1000 physical therapists - just like you - increase their wealth in a variety of ways.

In addition to holding a doctorate in physical therapy, Dr. Smith holds a Masters Degree in Public Health and is only 3 semesters away from earning a law degree (Juris Doctorate) at the time of writing this book. He uses his extensive knowledge as a business consultant to help many clients. His clients include those that are starting a business, those that are scaling a business, those wanting to learn how to trade in financial markets, those needing guidance in optimizing patient revenue cycles, and those needing regulatory guidance navigating federal law in their business(es).

Chapter 1: Growing Up

My full name is Robert Brandon Smith, but my whole life I have gone by my middle name, Brandon. If you ever have kids please save them the annoyance of having to explain to the school system, friends, and everyone why their legal first name is different from the name they go by.

I was born in Allentown, PA, but raised mostly in Naples, FL. My dad was a very successful surgeon, but unfortunately he left my mom when I was less than 2 years old. Therefore, for the most part, I was raised in a single-mother low-income household.

What was interesting about this dynamic is that I got to see two very different sides of the wealth spectrum growing up. Even though my mom worked very hard to support us, we always struggled. Because I lived with my mom, I attended public school, and due to her income, I qualified for financial assistance programs growing up (e.g. Free lunch from the public school system). When I tell people I grew up in Naples, they assume I was rich, but that couldn't be farther from the truth. Also, fuck those people.

Now my dad did well financially, but he seemed to get out of sending child support regularly, and would often say that he sent it when he did not.

However, when I would spend time with my dad - which was rare - he had a "have whatever you want, buy whatever you want" lifestyle, and it was downright obnoxious at times.

I do not know exactly when my dad remarried, as he was absent most of my life, but his remarriage led to me having a step-mom and eventually two step-brothers, Alex and Chris. Alex is my half brother, and Chris was adopted during my father's second marriage. For some reason, my dad also named them with a first name they never went by, and growing up they were also called by their middle names. Alex eventually just gave up explaining that he goes by his middle name to others and now just goes by his first name Jon to newer people in his life.

Now that you have some basic background information of my family dynamic and what it was like for me growing up, let's fast forward several years.

Chapter 2: The Unknown Struggle

Essentially, I did a lot of things and went through a lot of hardships before I became a PT.

In 2007, my dad died, one year later my stepmom died, and seven months after that my mom died. Yes, you read that correctly, 3 dead parents in less than 2 years.

Additionally, between the time of my dad's and stepmom's death, I was enlisted in the US Navy as an Air Rescue Swimmer/Aviation Warfare Operator - a relatively unknown component of the special warfare teams. I completed boot camp in Chicago, IL and aircrew school (which has a 50% attrition rate) in Pensacola, FL. After aircrew school, I then went on to air rescue swimmer school (Also in Pensacola, FL.).

Unfortunately, I was medically discharged during air rescue swimmer school. Part of me regrets that I did not get to continue being part of the naval special warfare teams, however, that discharge actually worked out better for me in the long run in so many ways.

Anyway, back to the story. Between the ages of 19 and 20, I was basically left on my own with no help from anyone. I was left with animals to take care of and estates to settle with literally zero guidance. My stepbrothers, who were 12 & 5 when my dad died, went to live with my stepmom's mom in another state. My mom had never remarried, and growing up we managed, but realistically, her income did not get far in a single-mother household.

My mom's death fucked me up, not only because she was my last surviving parent, but because it was unexpected. We had just celebrated her birthday a few days earlier. I had spoken to her on the phone earlier that day, and I was headed home to spend time with her.

Unfortuantely, that did not go as planned.

When I arrived at my mom's house, EMS and police were outside, and I was confused as fuck. The first thought I had was *well this can't be for me*. I thought this because we lived in a townhome, so I thought one of my neighbors was having an issue. Additionally, I think our minds protect us from the things we do not want to believe when the trauma is too real and unexpected.

As I walked up to my mom's house, a cop who was standing outside walked up to me and told me my mom was dead, without any warning whatsoever. The officers then handed me my Golden Retriever, Reef. I sat outside with my dog as they put my mom in a body bag and wheeled her body away on a stretcher to go to the Collier County morgue.

That moment felt surreal as fuck.

One day you're celebrating your mom's birthday with her, and with no warning whatsoever, a few days later she's gone.

DR. R. BRANDON SMITH

After sitting in shock for a while with my dog, my neighbor, Joe, who I had grown up with, came over to try and help in any way he could. We then went into my mom's house together.

I clearly was not okay, and the harsh reality wouldn't hit me until a few days later.

What they don't tell you is that whenever a body is taken away, the cops do not clean up the surrounding area. The cause of my mom's death was later determined to be a pulmonary embolism. Unfortunately, there was blood all over the floor from her pulmonary embolism that I had to clean up. Thankfully, my neighbor helped me.

I didn't know what to do or who to turn to.

I will tell you firsthand that those that need help the most are usually the least likely to ask for it… I started doing hard drugs for a bit, but stayed in school the whole time, because I thought at that time that was the only way to get ahead. I originally went to a community college after my military discharge, then transferred to an instate public university after earning an AA and ended up earning a BA in Biology in 2012. It took longer than expected, because I was also working 40 hours a week and supporting myself.

Upon undergrad graduation I realized that I could only deliver food with my BA in Biology. It became apparently clear that I had essentially played a joke on myself by pursuing a science degree with no transferable real world skills.

I then decided to look into graduate schools as I shadowed a variety of providers, but still couldn't say yes to one.

Making things more difficult is that my grades were shitty due to the struggles I went through.

I never had a true college experience because I only ever supported myself and mostly lived on my own while working through college.

Looking back now, that was probably better for me, as I was clearly fucked up in many ways and had my own issues to work through first, that many people will never be able to relate to.

Unfortunately, GPA is a screening part of any graduate application, and I would not even be able to tell my story to any admissions committee due to my GPA. I did take some post bac classes to increase my GPA, and even took an MCAT since I had the pre requisite classes for med school, as they were required for my degree, but most of the damage had already been done.

I ended up applying for an MPH thinking it was a long shot and luckily I was accepted. Due to the hybrid format, I actually finished that degree in about a year. My capstone project focused on fitness and nutrition, as it was clear I had an interest in that realm, but my path was not clear yet.

Note: A dual degree MPH/ PT is not useful in PT at all - building a business

is much more useful than any degree!

I had a biology degree, a masters degree, and an interest in healthcare, but looking back now what I really wanted was to find something where I was able to make ~100k a year and fuck around on YouTube etc… Essentially what I truly wanted was to use my degree to fund my other interests and eventually work for myself.

I continued to shadow a lot of providers in various settings.

The MPH landed me a job in clinical trials, which was better than my food delivery job.

However, after a while of doing the trials, I realized that a lot of the trials we were conducting were not actually medically necessary and that the job was super boring.

The truth is that the Fitness and PT industry can help individuals with lifestyle changes rather than medications. Sadly, many medications are used because people refuse to be accountable for their poor lifestyle choices. Hell, I even got fat during undergrad, because I couldn't put the fork down after my mom's death, but there's no doubt I was the one making poor lifestyle decisions.

Sometimes medication is medically necessary, but most health problems can be solved through proper diet, exercise, and accountability.

After a lot of back and forth and not feeling challenged in my clinical trials job, I decided to apply to PT school. I ended up submitting a PTCAS application only one time and getting into the University of Miami for PT school. I graduated in May 2018.

Ironically, earning a DPT caused me to become extremely poor...

Chapter 3:
A New Grad Nightmare

In 2018, I graduated from PT school and took a "Home Health" job in Tampa, FL.

But this job was pure fuckery.

I was promised 90k on my offer letter, but when I started, I was making nowhere near that amount.

Legal tip: If you're in a similar situation where you know your employer

knowingly made a fraudulent offer to you, you can sue them for fraudulent misrepresentation.

Anyway, back to the point. I was so broke at one point that all of my credit cards were maxed out. I could not afford food, I had no support from anyone, and I was literally stealing cookies from ALFs and scrounging for quarters in my car to buy food.

Not what I expected after earning a DPT!

Fed up, I decided to look more into Part A reimbursement and HH company structure.

Unfortunately, I had been scammed by a predatory staffing agency. These staffing agencies act as unnecessary middlemen that prey on new graduates and uninformed PTs!

I did not earn a doctorate to get fucked.

I have been through enough already, so I have a low tolerance for anything that does not value my time/education/etc...

The day I reached my breaking point, the owner asked me to commit medicare fraud or be fired because they couldn't keep census (patients on caseload).

It was at that moment that I decided to quit. The owner then threatened to report me to the state board for patient abandonment. However, legally, the continuity of care falls on the company, and not individual providers, so I finished all of my notes and peaced the fuck out. Additionally, I forwarded any threats to my personal email for my own records and legal records if necessary.

Legal Tip: If you finish all of your notes, you do not owe anyone anything and cannot be reported for patient abandonment. You can also file a lawsuit

against any employer who makes threats for retaliation.

The day after I resigned, I decided to apply for travel therapy jobs. Why? Because my classmates who did travel out of school were making significantly more than me, and since I no longer had an income, I had to do something.

As I was searching and inquiring about travel jobs in a few facebook groups, I was messaged by someone who was the director of a local home health agency that needed a PT. Ironically, his agency had worked with my now prior employer and hated them.

Due to my experience working in "Home Health", and our mutual hatred for my prior employer, I was offered an interview.

After the interview, and only 3 months after graduating, I had **my first offer for a $100,000.00 salary as a Home Health PT** at a medicare certified agency.

Hire Date:	October 9, 2018
Job Classification:	**PROFESSIONAL**
Job Title:	Physical Therapist
Annual Salary:	$100,000.00 ($48.08 hourly equivalent)
FLSA:	Exempt
Status:	Full-time
Schedule:	Minimum 40 hours per week
Travel:	As needed
Continuing Education:	Discretionary
Employee Benefits:	First of the month following 60-days of employment; January 1, 2019
Paid Time Off:	Diamond PTO policy, attached
Mileage Reimbursement:	.40 per mile

Chapter 4:
The Foundations
That Led
To Success

After securing a real home health offer (which I define as any offer 100k or above), I started telling my story on YouTube and explaining how predatory companies - like the one I previously worked for - are not necessary at all.

Unfortunately, there are a lot of them in PT. For some unknown reason, the old business model is to prey on new graduates and those that do not know any better…

Schools have no idea about this, and if they do, ironically a professor usually owns the company. This business model is outdated and predatory, and if you learn one thing from this book - let it be that **you can pay people well AND have a profitable and ethical business.**

Within a month of telling my story on YouTube, my subscriber count was growing and there was now a demand for a Home Health Course.

As I told my story on YouTube and created a course around the topic, it was very apparent that I was not the only one who had been taken advantage of by these predatory agencies. I eventually created a FB group as well, and launched the 10 CEU Home Health Mentor course. As more and more people took my course, they learned to cut these agencies out and go directly to legitimate agencies, and many of my students started getting even higher pay packages than I had.

Some of my students have earned over 200k - even as new grad Physical Therapists! Currently, I have helped over

1000 PTs earn 120k on average from my course alone, which is more than $120,000,000 going to PTs.

This was just the beginning. Now I do a lot more than sell courses. At the time you are reading this book, I will likely be earning around 20k a month on the low end. This monthly income is earned by doing a variety of things, including helping PTs just like you make their first $1000 online and more! You can read more about what I do in the about the author section in the beginning of this book.

This is just a brief overview of the foundation that led to my current success.

I hope that you can use this book as a roadmap (or at the very least, inspiration) to reach your goals.

If you need even more guidance, you can apply to my Inner Circle coaching program via the link or the QR code on the next page.

INNER CIRCLE APPLICATION LINKS AND QR CODE

https://bit.ly/3TgNf2W

Chapter 5: Money Matters

Many of you, whether it was growing up, in school, or working in the workplace, have been told not to talk about money. It has been consistently reinforced to you that "money is bad!" or "money is evil."

Thankfully, that narrative is just not true.

You need to talk about money and you need to use money to not only buy your time back, but also to elevate what you can do for yourself and for other people.

Contrary to popular belief - money does solve problems!

Now, if you are a good person, having extra money is going to amplify the amount of good that you can do. If you're a bad person, it's going to amplify the amount of bad or shitty things that you can do. I know many of you reading this are probably good people, so we're going to focus on that.

You want more money so that you can have more time for yourself, for your family, and have more freedom overall. You don't want to be stuck at a job that you hate because of financial issues.

When I graduated PT school in 2018, I didn't understand money that well, I had a really shitty job, and I was barely getting by.

As a Doctor of Physical Therapy, I was so fucking broke that I wasn't able to buy food regularly. I was scraping for change in my car to buy one item a day from a gas station, and I was stealing cookies from the ALFs (Assisted Living Facilities) that I was working in. All of the time and money that I had spent on the doctoral degree that led me to this situation put me in a very dark place. I thought about killing myself because I had no one, and I thought at that time that

ending it all would fix my problems… Thankfully, I'm too much
of a pussy to act on any of those
thoughts. Mainly because I had
recently adopted a cat, Carbon,
that I knew I needed to take care
of. He was my only family at
that time.

Whether people admit it or
not, I guarantee you that these
thoughts go through anyone's
head who has actually struggled-
especially when they do not see
a solution in sight. Even more
so when there is no support system. So, if you are having these
thoughts, do not act on them,
seek out people who have had it
worse off than you and succeeded

and let them show you the solutions that you may be blind to.

Additionally, you must understand that you are supposed to suffer before you achieve anything worthwhile.

What I've come to learn is that depression and discontentment are supposed to motivate you - you don't need drugs or a diagnosis - you need to man or women the fuck up and take control or your life.

You need to use discontentment, depression, unhappiness, etc… to motivate you to build the type of life that you want!

My unhappiness motivated me to leave a shitty job and find a six-figure PT job that solved many of my problems!

My first six-figure job was literally a catalyst that changed the trajectory of my life.

The new level of income allowed me to pay my bills on time, it allowed me to be able to afford food, it allowed me to stop struggling. More importantly, it allowed me to create my online business and teach others how to earn six-figures as employees. It started the process of growth that allowed me to get to where I am in life today. It also allowed me to join a gym and meet my wife!

This is why money matters!

Chapter 6:
PDGM LAYOFF

Even though I went from being broke to making 100k a year, and have helped other people do the same, it was not all an uphill success.

When PDGM occurred, I was actually laid off for being the highest paid employee at the company that had paid me so well.

Thankfully, due to my income, my online business, and my accountability for my own life, I was okay during that layoff.

I would like to mention that before laying me off, they did offer me a DOR position that caused me to drive my cat across the state of FL for literally no reason. However, this DOR position was a joke and a waste of my time. I was laid off shortly after starting the DOR position due to my salary package being too high and for refusing to "suck off' physicians for referrals.

After being laid off, I took an OP travel contract in Eufaula, Alabama. This contract was canceled ~6 weeks in due to COVID. I then switched to being a PRN Home Health PT working FT hours and weekends in Dothan,

AL. This whole time - even after being laid off, after PDGM, and during COVID - I was able to increase my income from zero to over 140k a year because I sought out opportunities and was willing to put in the work.

Chapter 8: Standards

Now I work 24/7 as a self-employed entrepreneur, but it all started with me getting a high paying job. I then used that high pay rate as my standard for the bare minimum that I would accept to be paid to work as a PT.

Guess what? You do not need to get a high paying job first for it to be your standard!

You can determine your standard now by designing the life you want and only accepting what aligns with the life you want!

A Home Health, Travel or a PRN position is the fastest way to make 6 figures as an employee, once you have your standards set.

To earn even more, you may want to consider opening a cash pay practice or any other business.

There are lots of resources for these options in the Outside The Box Income and Investing private discord, my courses, and my coaching program.

But back to the point on why you need to set standards for yourself!

You need to understand that if your needs are not being met financially, you are not going to be able to help anyone else.

You're going to be stressed out.

You're probably going to get fired or have some toxic relationship with your employer when you feel undervalued.

You're not going to be able to help your patients because you are not able to take care of yourself.

So, you need to get or create a source of income that aligns with the life you want first.

Now for those of you that say, "I was told to take a new grad rate. I don't have experience." My response to that is fuck that "let's make excuses and act like a whiny little bitch" mentality.

If you're reading this book - you're not taking a new grad rate.

Why? Because your license bills the same as somebody with a hundred years of experience. Just because somebody has years of experience doesn't mean that the insurance company is going to pay them more than somebody who graduates tomorrow.

DR. R. BRANDON SMITH

At the end of the day, if you're working in an insurance based setting, experience doesn't fucking matter.

You need to have a standard and only negotiate at or above the standard that you set.

This is how you get ahead in life.

Please understand that by accepting some shitty offer just because everyone else does, or your professor didn't teach you, or you just don't know about finance, that your acceptance of that offer is 100% your fault.

In order to be successful, you need to really embrace what I'm telling you.

Without embracing these concepts, you're going to be one of the new graduates I've talked to who has spent $135,000 to $200,000 plus on PT school with a first job offer of $22 an hour.

The sad reality is that if they didn't talk to me, they may have taken it.

I don't want that to be anybody reading this book and if it currently is you - I suggest that you quit immediately, because you'll get a higher ROI betting on yourself. At the end of the day, we all know that your shitty job does not line up with your own standards - so stop lying to yourself.

Chapter 8:
A Better Money Mindset On Student Loans

Note: This does not apply to private loans and you should pay private loans off as soon as possible.

It is not an accomplishment to pay off $200,000 of federal student loan debt in two years.

You may think it is, but it's not. Why? Because federal loans go away when you die.

So why the fuck are you throwing money at an asset that dies with you?

Sadly, people have thrown 200 plus into federal loans over two years. They could have invested that money instead, whether that's regular stocks, meme stocks, real estate, crypto, etc. They worked hard and by paying off student loans, they have basically thrown all of that money away.

They may have peace of mind now, but think about it this way: If they would have invested in Tesla and paid the minimum fed loan repayment on an IBR (Income

Based Repayment) plan, they'd probably have made around $1 million, after tax 700,000. With that $700,000 they could easily pay off the remaining amount and still have $500,000 left over.

Just something to consider.

If you are interested in learning more about investing and would like to join an investing tier of the Outside The Box Community, but do not want the weekly coaching that comes with the Inner Circle membership, go to the following link or scan the QR code below.

https://rbrandonsmith.
com/3ExGPZc

Chapter 9: Exposure

What you're exposed to can greatly determine what you believe your reality to be or what you believe you can achieve. Once you're exposed to it, you learn that it's possible, not only for other people, but for you too!

I'll use myself as an example. Many of you saw in June I turned a ~$1600 into over $180,000 via AMC out the money call options.

I don't share that with you to brag, and I didn't when I posted it in June, or when I repost it to show you what I did.

I share it with you to show you that it's possible.

Had I not known about out of the money options, risk management, and placing a true Wall Street bet, I wouldn't have been able to do it.

However, I was exposed to it so I knew it was possible for me.

I do want to clarify that I'm not telling you to go and do options trades like that unless of course you're in my Inner Circle coaching program where we discuss the market(s) every Tuesday and Wednesday morning at 8AM central.

However, I do want to use that as an example for when you take a little bit of risk and you get exposure to what's possible, you too can achieve what you're seeing other people achieve.

Another example is from when I was a PT student. During my last year of PT school, I did remote nutrition coaching for an online nutrition and fitness company. This position allowed me to observe backend data of the company and see that even with a very small team, the company was making $150,000 a week!

This is possible for anyone who sets large goals and is consistent over time.

You must realize that there are people out there just like you running very small companies making 150K a week. It is possible for you too!

You just have to be exposed to it and learn from people who have done what you want to do.

Now I've made a lot of money from options trading and I've made 40K in one week from my 10 CEU Home Health Course via an email sequence in June 2021.

I will tell you as someone that's been on academic probation multiple times, gotten C's most of my life, and struggled- if I can do it, so can you.

I share these things with you because I want you to know that it's possible.

That being said, there are things you have to do that most people are not willing to do or not willing to pay to learn how to do.

These things include building an audience, making the right connections, building the right product, pricing product(s) appropriately, meeting the right people, etc…

But you cannot begin to implement a strategy if you do not know what your end result looks like.

The first and most important thing you need to do to get ahead in life is expose yourself to new possibilities and surround yourself with people who are doing what you want to do!

You're always taking a risk when you step outside of your comfort zone, but you want to take risks that are going to expose you to more than what you currently know.

Example: Many people who have joined the private community have started trading options by watching the live Q and As and have seen 80% gains on their first options trade. They didn't know that was possible before.

So go out there and expose yourself - not in the misdemeanor/felony way, but go out there and expose yourself to things that are going to increase your value, increase your net worth, increase your network, and ultimately increase what you can do for others.

And you need to do that today.

If I didn't do any of the things that I did, I would probably just be a miserable PT complaining all of the time, whining, bitching, and moaning "oh poor me", essentially not being accountable for where I'm at currently in life. The majority of PTs fall into this bitch made category - don't let yourself be one of them.

You can't just sit there, whine, bitch, and moan, and expect results. Especially when you haven't even started or have not been consistently working towards a goal over a long enough period.

You can create the life you want or you can settle for mediocrity…

Chapter 10:
Time Is Your Most
Valuable Asset

You have to understand that time is your most valuable asset.

If you're consistently trading time for money in a way that doesn't value you, you're going to burn out, you're going to hate your life, and the people around you are not going to like you either.

You've been raised to go to school, where you trade your time for an education that teaches you how to trade your time for money - AKA be the best employee that you can be.

Then, you either go into the workforce or you continue on in school, where you pay exorbitant amounts of money for knowledge, as you lose time learning how to be a higher skilled employee. This is clearly evidenced by the fact that schools market employment rates. You have to realize right now that anytime you let someone else determine your worth, you're doing a disservice to yourself.

You must determine your own worth before you do anything.

You could die tomorrow, you could get hit by a truck, you could have a bad medical diagnosis. And ideally, wherever you are right now, whatever you're working on, or whatever you're around or whoever you're around, you want to leave that environment, that person, whatever it is, better than when you arrived in that situation.

The reason I've done the majority of things I've done is to leave the PT profession better than I found it. Additionally, providing massive value to others has also allowed me to create a better life for myself and my family.

But, it's up to you. You could be like, "Hey, fuck everybody, I don't care." That's totally okay. As long as you're honest with yourself and that's who you are, that's cool.

Honesty is always going to earn respect more than lying.

But back to my main point on why time matters.

You need to value your time, whether it's your education, whether it's a trade, whether it's a skill, whatever it is, you need to value it appropriately.

Because if you continue to go to work for somebody who is paying you much less than what you're valued, much less than your colleagues, you're going to get burned out, you're going to get pissed off, you're going to become resentful.

This resentment should piss you off and motivate you at the same time. It should motivate you to create a system that works for you.

If a system does not work for you or it does not support you, you need to create your own system.

That's exactly what I did, how I make money online, why I created online courses, and why I've built a mentorship community. I've also done things through investing, but you really want to be in control of your own income. The best way to do that is to create a system that works for you.

Investing in yourself is the first step!

For most people, that's going to be building an online, in-person, or hybrid business.

It becomes even easier when you have a partner that truly loves and supports you.

I accomplished a lot on my own, but I accomplished even more since meeting my wife.

Why?

Because she supports me, she understands my goals. You want to have a partner that under-stands you. But that being said, you have to be self driven and motivated first.

You are what you attract - so be successful first.

Work when others aren't and the universe will reward you.

Pro Tip: If your wife/husband/transgender pronoun person does not love or support you - get a new one - they are holding you back from living the life that you know you can build for yourself.

The main point is that you need to value your time and you need to be driven. And if you're not driven and you're not valuing your time, then nobody's responsible for where you currently are in life but you.

Some of you may be like, "Hey, I want to make 40K in a week, like you did. Hey, I want to start an online course, like you did."

Then just fucking start!

Stop saying things like, "Oh well, I need it to be 32 degrees on a Tuesday, I need it to be sunny, there needs to be a beaver that walks across my yard that day, and that's when I will start my business." That's not going to happen.

If your business is conditional, then your success is conditional.

Speed is always going to win.

So if you're thinking about starting a business, just start.

If you need your hand held and a community to keep you accountable - join the Inner Circle coaching program:

https://bit.ly/3TgNf2W

Chapter 11:
Fuck The Haters

I started putting out content years ago and yes, it is true that people are going to get mad at you and/or people are going to hate you.

I get messages all the time that say, "Hey, fuck you. Hey, get out of PT." I know it's because I'm doing better than they are and people don't criticize anyone doing worse than them.

You have to realize that people are only criticizing you because they don't want you to be better off than they are, or they subconsciously feel that you're better than they are and feel threatened. They do not hold any power in or accountability for their own lives.

Again, no one doing better than you is going to criticize you.

Additionally, you may have been fear mongered away from starting a business by classmates, schools, professional organizations, and even told that your idea is illegal by people who do not know what the fuck they are talking about. Realistically, take a look at their lives and think if you really want your life to look like theirs... I guarantee you that answer is no.

High performers only want others to succeed, low performers want to suck on mommy or daddy's titty and blame others for their problems.

Embrace the hate because it's a sign of success.

Chapter 12:
How To Make
$100,000.00 -
$200,000.00
Plus Annually
As An Employee

Here's my first real Home Health Offer

Hire Date:	October 9, 2018
Job Classification:	**PROFESSIONAL**
Job Title:	Physical Therapist
Annual Salary:	$100,000.00 ($48.08 hourly equivalent)
FLSA:	Exempt
Status:	Full-time
Schedule:	Minimum 40 hours per week
Travel:	As needed
Continuing Education:	Discretionary
Employee Benefits:	First of the month following 60-days of employment; January 1, 2019
Paid Time Off:	Diamond PTO policy, attached
Mileage Reimbursement:	.40 per mile

Some of you reading this are probably thinking I'm full of shit or that only I've done this. To crush that doubt here is a testimonial from a PT I helped make over 213k in 11 months as a new grad!

"As a new grad, many people told me that I would only make a specific amount because that was normal. Until I took the home health mentor course, I was convinced that to be true. Brandon told me everything that I know about how to get paid effectively and know my worth. His guidance was invaluable and my return on my investment from taking his course and learning how to operate properly was amazing. Case in point- in 11 months, I earned $213,000, on track to make 230k at the end of the year as A STAFF PHYSICAL THERAPIST. I attribute a vast majority of this salary that is well over twice the average salary of a physical therapist to the course and I especially appreciated the ongoing support that the Facebook group that is exclusive to course alumni for constant updates in how to navigate the ever-changing course of home health. I cannot emphasize this enough, this course changed my life and I was able to pay off all of my debt in one year." - Rahul Rikhy PT, DPT

This is why I do what I do, to have impact like this and help others on a massive scale in many ways!

Go to the link on the next page to see more testimonials and to purchase the 10 CEU Home Health Course yourself.

Use Code HIDDENINCOME for 80% OFF (Over $1600 OFF!)

https://rbrandonsmith. com/3TgaGJQ

Rahul is not the only physical therapist I've helped earn over 200k and home health is not the only setting physical therapists I've worked with have achieved this in.

The settings that can most likely allow you to earn 100-200k/year as an employee PT are cash pay, home health, and travel. Business ownership may be included here, but you will reach this goal faster if you are working on your business and not in your business.

What makes PTs who reach 100-200k in income different from the status quo of burned out shitty PTs?

They seek out opportunities and have a desire to thrive.

Currently, we live in Mississippi and I still go on interviews as research for my New

Grad Negotiation Course and I once again have had offers in the 113k + range.

If I can do it in the deep south, you can do it anywhere.

I do want you to note that making real money as an employee will burn you out. However, if you need capital, being an employee is the best option to start. This is how I started.

Additional Resources Relevant To This Chapter:

Go here to travel with a travel company I trust:

**https://rbrandonsmith.
com/3Cvprlu**

Use my affiliate link here to check out Aaron Lebauers Cash PT Blueprint Course to start a six figure cash practice from $0!

https://rbrandonsmith. com/3RZM8Uv

The New Grad Negotiation Course is free for my coaching clients, but you can also grab a copy here:

https://rbrandonsmith. com/3g7yzoy

Chapter 13:
How to Make
$100,000.00
USD Online in
Passive Income

Before anyone says, "I don't believe you", attached is my third party verification of earning over 100k from one product alone - The 10 CEU Home Health Mentor Course™. Additionally, at the time of this writing I have also earned over 250k online, so to clarify, I know what the fuck I am talking about.

Please do not listen to anyone who has no social proof of what they are teaching you. I

am begging you - always thoroughly vet anyone you are learning from or planning to learn from.

So how do you make $100k in passive income? You follow these steps:

Step 1: Identify a problem

Step 2: Figure out what the most common issues are surrounding the problem that you identified

Step 3: Identify the rules around the problem - whether they are personal, societal, or both

Step 4: Analyze how you can solve at least one of the issues surrounding the problem utilizing or breaking the rules that you have identified

Step 5: Create your offer as an outcome for what someone gets or achieves when they work with you, buy your product, etc…

Step 6: Sales

Step 7: Systems

Step 8: Marketing

How did I use this system to make my first 100k online?

The problem I identified to make was two-fold.

The first part being that PTs on a massive scale - especially new grads - were being taken advantage of.

How did I know this was a problem? It is exactly what happened to me.

The second part of the problem was the huge discrepancy in PT pay for Home Health Therapists between those that work at predatory staffing agencies and legitimate home health agencies.

I used Kajabi to create my offer, created a Stripe account to process payments(systems), and I marketed direct-to-consumer via YouTube.

It is honestly not hard, but too many people get stuck on the small steps so that they cannot see the bigger picture.

If you would like me to help you get unstuck, apply here:

https://bit.ly/3TgNf2W

Chapter 14: How to Make $10,000.00 USD a Month In Recurring Revenue

Currently between my courses and The Outside Box Income and Investing Community™ I created - I generate around 20k a month at the time of this writing. However, it did not start that way. Before you even think about starting a monthly recurring revenue service ,you must have an audience and be proven in that space.

So how do you capture or create an audience?

You must identify issues in something that you are interested in and then present solutions on how to resolve those issues on a large platform.

More thorough steps were just discussed in the previous chapter, so hopefully you're not reading the book out of order. But if you are, refer to the previous chapter.

What platform should you use to capture an audience?

For organic leads, I highly recommend YouTube. YouTube is owned by Google, and therefore is a search engine. TikTok and Instagram are great, but no one is searching for content on those platforms. That being said, if you have a large audience on Instagram or TikTok, then you need to get them on your email list - TODAY!

If you do not have an email list, then you need to create one as soon as possible.

I personally use the PT Email Engine

You can try it for $1!

**https://rbrandonsmith.
com/3EDD6cP**

However, I started with Kajabi and SendFox. There are a lot of free platforms out there like mailerlite, mailchimp, etc....

You can also try 30 days of Kajabi on me by going here:

https://rbrandonsmith.
com/3Treet3

Chapter 15:
How to Make Money in the Stock Market

Below is my best trade of 2021. I turned $1678.00 into $151,023.00 by buying OTM Call Options. This was done via options trading, but do not worry, we are not going to start you there. If you want to learn more about options trading, I teach this in the Outside The Box Income and Investing Private Community, as well as with my Inner Circle coaching clients.

Amount	Equity
+23	$152,674.00
Breakeven	Exp Date
$40.72	6/18
Current Price	Avg Cost
$66.38	$0.72
Today's Return	+$141,220.00 (+1,232.93%)
Total Return	+$151,023.00 (+9,147.37%)

Warning: Traditional PTs hate that I've done this, and will continue to - but then again, where are their trades...?

P.S. This is not my only 1000%+ trade either.

Before you even consider investing in any financial

market, you must understand that all markets are speculative. Never risk money you cannot afford to lose, and you will never go broke taking profits and setting stop-losses.

The safest way to make money is to buy shares in companies you believe in over the long term.

SPY has historically done well, as have Apple and Microsoft. These are safer plays in the market. However we are most likely either in a recession or headed for one at the time of writing this (2022), so this may be the time to learn the market or invest in your business instead.

October 14, 2022

Goose27 Today at 8:49 AM
Can't say enough about benefits of inner circle program... 11 winning trades in a row. Just made $216 in 15 min. I have literally doubled my trading account in 2 wks.

Chapter 16:
How to Make
Money in Crypto

Remember from the previ-ous chapter that all markets are speculative. The easiest way to make money in Crypto is to hold long-term. The next best way is to buy during a bear-market and sell during a bull-market. An additional way to get to trade with 5-100x leverage and get massive returns in crypto is to trade crypto futures - this is something that I teach my Inner Circle coaching clients who have a high-risk tolerance, but I do not recommend that you start here.

Start with learning and understanding the crypto space first.

Without a strong foundation, you are guaranteed to lose money long term.

Most importantly, you need to determine if you are an investor or a trader.

Investors believe 1BTC=1BTC

Traders believe 1BTC = the market price

*BTC = Bitcoin

You can be both, or be a trader first, then an investor. However, you will not succeed if you do not know what you are doing and do not understand what you are doing.

If you need more guidance, join the tier of the Outside The Box Income and Investing Community that you feel is most appropriate for you.

https://rbrandonsmith.
com/3ExGPZc

Chapter 17: Real Estate

My biggest mistake after making massive gains in the stock and crypto markets was not investing in real estate.

Why did I not invest in real estate?

My wife is an Air Force physician, so we will most likely be moving a lot in the future. We agreed not to buy any property unless we know that we will be in an area for at least 3 years and that we can use a VA loan.

Most generational wealth is made in real estate. By owning a house, you can offset your taxes, and if you own a house and a business, you can rent your house to your business for 14 days under the Augusta Rule. So, if you rent your house to your business at $1000 a day for 14 days, you can pay yourself $14,000 tax-free.

Currently, I would be wary of any real estate purchase unless you fully understand the market that you are buying in, which means understanding interest rates, supply, demand, inflation and more.

Additionally, you must understand why you are buying the property.

If you do not understand these things, then it is not the right time for you to be buying a house.

Bonus #1: Takeaways

If you take away anything from this book, let it be the following concepts.

You may be addicted to comfort.

99% of people are afraid to start.

I encourage you to always choose growth over comfort.

You did not learn sales and marketing in school, therefore,

you are going to have to learn them yourself.

Perfection will kill your business faster than anything else. e.g. My first YouTube videos were trash, but people cared about the message.

It is okay to fail, as long as you fail forward.

As of 2022, if you are not earning at least 8.5% in a savings account, you are actually losing money due to inflation.

The best hedge against inflation is multiple sources of income - especially investments that outperform inflation. BUT

- you must maximize one source of income first!

Ultimately, success is determined by how consistent you can be over time - even when there is no short term ROI.

Bonus #2: Three Things You Should Never Feel Guilty About Spending Money On.

1. Hiring a business coach - hiring someone who's ahead of you to coach you will accelerate your speed.

2. Experiences - You can never get time or experiences back. Do not feel guilty prioritizing these. Some of your best

business/ income ideas may happen when you embrace this concept.

3. Whatever is going to help you take care of yourself mentally, physically, etc…

Bonus #3:
Three Keys
To Success

Believe in yourself

Do the work even when it's hard and you feel like giving up

Never let anyone's judgment get to you

Where To Find/ Contact Me

ALL PRODUCT LINKS CREATED THUS FAR CAN BE FOUND HERE:

https://campsite.bio/
drsmithdpt

APPLY FOR INNER CIRCLE COACHING:

https://drsmithdpt.
clickfunnels.com/

application-page
1653662356630

OUTSIDE THE BOX INCOME AND INVESTING PRIVATE COMMUNITY:

https://www.patreon.
com/drsmithdpt

10 CEU HOME HEALTH MENTOR COURSE:

https://homehealth
mentor.mykajabi.
com/

Instagram: https://
www.instagram.com/
dr.smith_dpt/

YouTube: https://
www.youtube.com/
channel/
UChZwdSCnzOG
Ghcl2hbt2Iwg

EMAIL:

brandon@outsidethe
boxincomeand
investing.com

Testimonials

"Dr. Smith's coaching provided knowledge, encouragement and accountability to help me launch my 1st online course and make >$1000 in sales in the 1st month! He also educated me about how to confidently invest in crypto when I had trepidations about the risks of the crypto market."

Dr. Phillip Magee, PT, DPT, GCS

"Brandon's guidance is definitely worth the money and saved me time/aggravation!"

Dr. Jillian Meyer, PT, DPT, WCS, CLT-LANA

I grew my initial investment of $1500 to $10,000 this year from Dr. Smith's recommendations!

Dr. Akash Patel PT, DPT

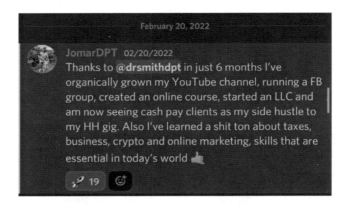

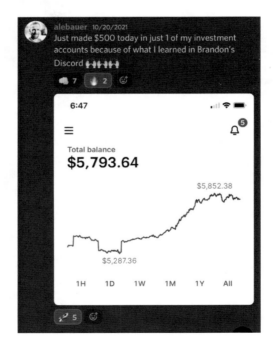

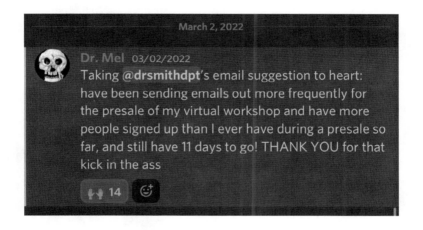

Dr. Mel 03/02/2022
Taking @drsmithdpt's email suggestion to heart: have been sending emails out more frequently for the presale of my virtual workshop and have more people signed up than I ever have during a presale so far, and still have 11 days to go! THANK YOU for that kick in the ass

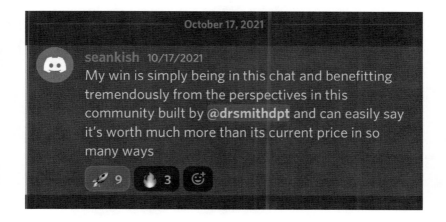

ALL PRODUCT LINKS CREATED THUS FAR CAN BE FOUND HERE:

https://campsite.bio/ drsmithdpt